CELEBRATING HOLIDAYS

Kwanzaa

by Rachel Grack

BLASTOFF! READERS
2

BELLWETHER MEDIA • MINNEAPOLIS, MN

Note to Librarians, Teachers, and Parents:

Blastoff! Readers are carefully developed by literacy experts and combine standards-based content with developmentally appropriate text.

Level 1 provides the most support through repetition of high-frequency words, light text, predictable sentence patterns, and strong visual support.

Level 2 offers early readers a bit more challenge through varied simple sentences, increased text load, and less repetition of high-frequency words.

Level 3 advances early-fluent readers toward fluency through increased text and concept load, less reliance on visuals, longer sentences, and more literary language.

Level 4 builds reading stamina by providing more text per page, increased use of punctuation, greater variation in sentence patterns, and increasingly challenging vocabulary.

Level 5 encourages children to move from "learning to read" to "reading to learn" by providing even more text, varied writing styles, and less familiar topics.

Whichever book is right for your reader, Blastoff! Readers are the perfect books to build confidence and encourage a love of reading that will last a lifetime!

This edition first published in 2017 by Bellwether Media, Inc.

No part of this publication may be reproduced in whole or in part without written permission of the publisher. For information regarding permission, write to Bellwether Media, Inc., Attention: Permissions Department, 5357 Penn Avenue South, Minneapolis, MN 55419.

Library of Congress Cataloging-in-Publication Data

Names: Koestler-Grack, Rachel A., 1973- author.
Title: Kwanzaa / by Rachel Grack.
Description: Minneapolis, MN : Bellwether Media, Inc., 2017. | Series:
    Blastoff! Readers: Celebrating Holidays | Includes bibliographical
    references and index. | Audience: Ages: 5-8. | Audience: Grades: K to
    Grade 3.
Identifiers: LCCN 2016034192 (print) | LCCN 2016035316 (ebook) | ISBN
    9781626175969 (hardcover : alk. paper) | ISBN 9781681033266 (ebook)
Subjects: LCSH: Kwanzaa–Juvenile literature. | African Americans–Social
    life and customs–Juvenile literature.
Classification: LCC GT4403 .K64 2017 (print) | LCC GT4403 (ebook) | DDC
    394.2612–dc23
LC record available at https://lccn.loc.gov/2016034192

Editor: Christina Leaf   Designer: Lois Stanfield

Printed in the United States of America, North Mankato, MN.

Table of Contents

Kwanzaa Is Here!

African cloths cover the table. The black candle glows in the *kinara*.

kinara

unity cup

After lighting the candle, the family drinks from a **unity** cup. Kwanzaa is here!

What Is Kwanzaa?

Kwanzaa honors African **culture** of the past, present, and future.

The name comes from the Swahili word *kwanza*, meaning "first fruits."

How Do You Say?

Word	Pronunciation
karamu	kah-RAH-moo
kinara	kee-NAR-ah
Kwanzaa	KWAHN-zah
mazao	mah-ZAH-oh
mkekas	em-KAY-kahz
zawadi	zah-WAH-dee

Who Celebrates Kwanzaa?

Kwanzaa began in the United States. Today, people across the world celebrate.

United States

African Americans remember their **heritage**. Other people can enjoy celebrations, too!

Dr. Maulana
Karenga

Dr. Maulana Karenga started Kwanzaa in 1966. He thought African Americans needed a time to celebrate their culture.

He based Kwanzaa **traditions** on African **harvest festivals**.

harvest festival,
Senegal

11

Time to Celebrate

Kwanzaa begins on December 26 and lasts for seven days.

The days have different **principles**. Families talk about the principle on that day.

Kwanzaa Traditions!

days

2 4 6 1 7 5 3

Families light a new kinara candle each night. Candle colors hold special meaning.

Black is for African heritage. Red stands for past struggles, and green is for hope.

Kwanzaa Candles

Day	Principle
1	Unity or togetherness
2	Speaking for yourself
3	Working together
4	Supporting one another
5	Having a purpose or goal
6	Creating something beautiful or helpful
7	Believing in yourself and others

People fill *mazao* baskets with fruits, vegetables, and nuts for decoration. The mazao includes an ear of corn for each child.

mazao

Mazao baskets sit on special mats called *mkekas*.

Families enjoy *karamu*, a feast of African foods, on day six. They play African music and dance. They celebrate being together.

Make a Kwanzaa Flag

You can celebrate Kwanzaa with a special flag!

What You Need:

- construction paper:
  - one red piece, cut 7 inches by 6 inches
  - one black piece, cut 7 inches by 4 inches
  - one green piece, cut 7 inches by 2 inches
- scissors
- pencil
- glue
- ¼-inch wooden dowel, cut 12 inches long
- tape

What You Do:

1. Glue the black paper onto the red paper so that the bottoms (longer side) and sides line up.
2. Glue the green piece on top of the black piece so that the bottoms and sides line up.
3. Punch a hole in the top left side of the flag and bottom left side of the flag.
4. Poke the dowel through the front of the lower hole and through the back of the upper hole.
5. Tape the back of the flag to the dowel to hold it in place.

1

4

5

People give each other *zawadi* on the last day. These special gifts are **symbols** of African culture.

Children learn about their heritage during Kwanzaa!

Glossary

culture—the traditions and way of life of a group of people

harvest festivals—celebrations of the farming season and the foods it produces

heritage—the history of a person or a group of people

principles—teachings or ideas

symbols—objects that stand for ideas or beliefs

traditions—customs, ideas, and beliefs handed down from one generation to the next

unity—togetherness

To Learn More

AT THE LIBRARY
Herrington, Lisa M. *Kwanzaa*. New York, N.Y.:
Children's Press, 2014.

Medearis, Angela Shelf. *Seven Spools of Thread: A Kwanzaa Story*. Morton Grove, Ill.: Albert Whitman, 2000.

Otto, Carolyn. *Celebrate Kwanzaa*. Washington, D.C., National Geographic, 2008.

ON THE WEB
Learning more about Kwanzaa
is as easy as 1, 2, 3.

1. Go to www.factsurfer.com.

2. Enter "Kwanzaa" into the search box.

3. Click the "Surf" button and you will see a
   list of related web sites.

With factsurfer.com, finding more
information is just a click away.

Index

The images in this book are reproduced through the courtesy of: Blend Images/ SuperStock, front cover (candles); VStock/ Alamy, front cover (fruit); Kwame Zikomo/ Purestock/ SuperStock, p. 4; Kwame Zikomo/ Purestock/ Alamy, pp. 4-5; AP Images, pp. 6-7, 10-11, 12-13; David Cooper/ Getty Images, pp. 8-9; Hemis/ Alamy, p. 11; Image Source/ SuperStock, p. 12; AvailableLight, pp. 14-15; CORBIS/ Age Fotostock, p. 16; Hill Street Studios/ Blend Images/ Newscom, pp. 16-17, 20-21; Shahar Azran/ Getty Images, p. 18; Lois Stanfield, p. 19 (all); Education Images/ Getty Images, p. 20; Kayte Deioma/ Alamy, p. 22.